THE JEWISH
SECRET

ALAN ASP

Copyright © 2018 by Alan Asp

THE JEWISHSECRET

All rights reserved. No part of this publication may be reproduced, distributed, or transmitted in any form or by any means, including photocopying, recording, or other electronic or mechanical methods, without the prior written permission of the publisher, except in the case of brief quotations embodied in critical reviews and certain other noncommercial uses permitted by copyright law. For permission requests, write to the publisher, addressed "Attention: Permissions Coordinator," at info@beyondpublishing.net

Quantity sales special discounts are available on quantity purchases by corporations, associations, and others. For details, contact the publisher at the address above.

Orders by U.S. trade bookstores and wholesalers. Email info@BeyondPublishing.net

The Beyond Publishing Speakers Bureau can bring authors to your live event. For more information or to book an event contact the Beyond Publishing Speakers Bureau speak@BeyondPublishing.net

The Author can be reached directly BeyondPublishing.net/AuthorAlanAsp

Manufactured and printed in the United States of America distributed globally by BeyondPublishing.net

New York | Los Angeles | London | Sydney

ISBN Softcover: 978-1-947256-60-6

ISBN Hardcover: 978-1-949873-87-0

I dedicate this book to my wife, Donna, who was an integral part of my journey to find myself. None of it would have happened without her love and encouragement. She is my rock.

CONTENTS

Chapter 1:   The Journey   07

Chapter 2:   Reshaping My View of Money   15

Chapter 3:   Money is More Important than Anyone   17

Chapter 4:   Honor Your Mother and Father   19

Chapter 5:   Be a Professional Giver   26

Chapter 6:   Living Within Your Means   32

Chapter 7:   Honor and Be At Peace with God   34

Chapter 8:   Be a professional Learner   40

Chapter 9:   Speak to Your Future   44

Chapter 10: Be a Master Networker   49

Chapter 11: Live to Eat Healthy   54

Chapter 12: It All Came Together   57

Chapter 1

THE JOURNEY

Taking stock of one's life is often a painful process. In 2009, I had no choice but to face the mess that had become my life. After a 17-year marriage, I had been divorced for two years and was supporting two kids. I wasn't dating anyone seriously mainly because I was too broke to take anyone on a date. I thought things were bleak but, at the time, had no realistic idea how bad it was until someone flat out asked me about my net worth. I was afraid to face the truth and forced myself to confront the situation head on. I had no money and no retirement. My net worth was $335,000 in the red. I hated what my life had become. I had lost my faith. I did not like my religion. I was alone, broke and buried in debt. I had burned my bridges with my family and friends. I owed them so much money that they refused to loan me anymore. My family told me they were sick of bailing me out. I was convinced that no one's financial life could get much worse than mine. I knew I needed to change.

My lowest point smacked me upside the head when I was making plans to go to my daughter's graduation in Massachusetts. I went through the motions to book a flight but then had no money to pay for an airline ticket. My attempt to reserve a hotel room failed because my credit cards were at their limit.

Coming up with what I thought was a brilliant idea, I decided I would drive the 700 miles to the graduation and once I got there, I'd save money by sleeping in a tent that I bought for $20 at the local hardware store. Needless to say, the trip was a disaster. It was hot. I was sweaty and eaten up by the bugs. The tent experiment went so badly that I finally just slept in my car. Even though I was grateful to have been able to see my daughter graduate, the depression I felt was overwhelming once I realized that I was not able pay for the simplest things in life.

Does anybody ever consciously decide to be in debt? The reason why debt is so overwhelming is because you're basically indebted to someone else and you have to live by their rules. If you can't make your mortgage payment, you can have your house taken away. If you do not make your car payment, then your vehicle can be repossessed. It is all a system of bondage.

Student loans are another form of bondage. I never planned on getting into student loan debt but wanting to help my daughter succeed, I co-signed on her student loan. I took the loan thinking I could just make the monthly payments and pay it off within five years. The initial loan was for $30,000 but by the time she left school two years later, the loan was roughly $33,000 with interest. So I started making payments but very quickly found out that nothing was coming off the principal until I repaid the interest. The bank told me that if I made the minimum payment amount monthly, I will pay back a total of $83,477.12 over 263 payments. Do the math. At that rate it was going to take 21 years to pay off that ball and chain.

I never read the fine print on the loan agreement. There is no end date on the life of the loan and the borrower pays compounded interest every month. The payback doesn't begin until the student is out of school. During the life of the loan, you can't get out of it or collect social security until the entire loan is paid in full.

This stunned me and I started making double payments that totaled over $700 a month. After a few months, I still hadn't made a dent in the interest to pay down the loan. I kept looking at this as a mountain that was nearly impossible to climb. I had hit rock bottom.

Paying off this loan became my number one goal in life. I took out another type of loan just to pay back the student loan. In an act of desperation I even went so far as to consult with a bankruptcy lawyer. He said forget it. You cannot get that one discharged even in bankruptcy. And, to make matters worse, my daughter wasn't in a position to help pay back the loan.

I desperately wanted to change from being in bondage to my bills and not enjoying my life at all. I think that is one of the worst things you could ever do is to get yourself into crushing debt. It's such a horrible experience. I was adding over $1,000 a month in debt every month that I am alive.

How is it possible to do that? Relying on credit cards, of course. Lots of people do it. They hear "24 months, no payments". They hear "easy credit". Most of us do it and quickly find ourselves living way above our means. I just had too much pride to stop the cycle.

I was living the so-called American dream. I wanted to enjoy my life while not facing the consequences. It all came to a screeching halt when the card companies stopped giving me credit. My family and friends stopped giving me loans. The credit cards I did have were maxed out and I found that the cards were the biggest contributor to the mountain of debt. Yet, I did not realize just how bad it was until I found myself living on canned corn and a loaf of white bread.

Sometimes as we look back at our life, we can see how events occurred that directed us to our true path. When I look back, I realize that my Jewish Journey was perfectly timed.

In 2009, while I was drowning in my debt and depression, I was an invited guest to the Bat Mitzvah of the daughter of my good friend, Danny Applefield and his wife, Lisa Walters. A Bat Mitzvah is a rite of passage, when a young Jewish girl turns twelve and takes on the rights and obligations of a Jewish adult, and realizes her place in the community. A Jewish boy will have his Bar Mitzvah at age 13 and like the Bat Mitzvah, he is considered an adult as well.

The occasion is marked by participation in the weekly Sabbath service. The weekly portion of the service takes an average of two years of study and is followed by a joyous celebration attended by family and friends of the celebrant.

The act of witnessing an event such as this was so very unique and quite odd to me. I had so many conflicting feelings and thoughts of what I might encounter in a Jewish synagogue. Being raised in a Christian home, it was ingrained in me to dislike Jews. They were cold and anti-Christian. As it turned out, every preconceived notion that I had of the Jewish experience was wrong.

I was fascinated while watching the confident young girl stand at the *bema*, which is the pulpit or platform, and recite the ritual prayers and weekly Torah portion in Hebrew in front of the congregation. The weekly Torah portion is a section of the Five Books of Moses used in the Jewish liturgy during a single week.

At the time I didn't realize that Hebrew was the only language that God gave to man. A modern day Jew learns to speak Hebrew in honor and reverence to God. In my Christian past I was taught that God gave the Hebrew language to Abraham as part of the covenant. I hadn't made the connection that the Hebrew language is a foundation of the Jewish faith.

All along the way, I always felt that I was a spiritual person and loved God with all my heart, soul and mind. I consciously lived as an honest and caring man and tried to do good deeds and serve as much as humanly possible. I can't explain it, but when I walked in Temple Israel that first time, something deep inside my soul was saying that I had found home. I struggled to understand the concept of "coming home" in this foreign place of worship, and the overwhelming feeling of being welcome that brought me to tears.

I have to say I was not looking for a new place of worship. After all I was a trained Pentecostal preacher, who has spoken to audiences over a thousand times.

Temple Israel soon became my spiritual home and I purposefully set out to learn everything I could about the Jewish people and their way of life. I joined the synagogue and enrolled in several courses to learn all I could about Judaism. I learned about serving God, the Written Word, and the significance of observing the Sabbath. I learned the prayers and studied the Jewish festivals and holidays. I learned that God loves me unconditionally and wants me to prosper.

And that was when I came to realize the Jewish way of life was the key to my future success.

Deep down I knew that the answer to what I was seeking was at this Jewish place but I didn't know where to begin. After meeting with one of the five rabbis' who lead this very large congregation, I started attending weekly Friday night Sabbath services. Soon that wasn't enough, so I started going to mid-week classes that were offered on various topics. I was hungry for even more, so I made the decision to convert.

During my ongoing counseling with Rabbi Marla Hornstein, (mhornstein@temple-israel.org) we focused on where I wanted to go with my newfound faith. It was a time of introspection and to reflect if conversion was truly what I wanted to do. There was absolutely no pressure and it turned into a very rewarding experience.

I need to point out that I was learning things that were never taught nor talked about during my four years at Southeastern Bible College in Lakeland, FL where I graduated with some amazing people like famed author and motivational speaker Jerry Grillo (www.liveit2win.com) as well as popular author and life coach Tim Storey (www.timstorey.com).

All I ever heard was Jesus was real and the Old Testament was not significant anymore. I was taught that God gave Christians a new covenant and we were no longer supposed to adhere to the old covenant or the Old Testament. As I started out on my Jewish Journey, I learned that the Old Testament is in fact real and not only relevant, but contains the wealth principles that guided my future success.

Before I go on, let me clarify that my Jewish Journey was truly all about finding my authentic spiritual self. It was a bonus to discover the wealth principles buried between the lines. I admit, I was attracted to the aspect of gaining prosperity as I was still struggling with my horrible financial situation. It goes hand and hand that to get this great wealth, you have to be at peace with God and that it is acceptable to have increase and prosperity.

*"But remember the Lord your God, for it is he who gives you the ability to produce wealth, and so confirms his covenant, which he swore to your ancestors, as it is today." (*Deuteronomy 8:18)

As I continued through the learning process, quite a few of my teachers were surprised that I used to be not only a Christian, but an Assembly of God minister as well. What they didn't understand was that I was on a spiritual journey, that I was spiritually incomplete. I was content being a Jew.

Jesus said, *"Don't suppose I came to do away with the Law and the Prophets. I did not come to do away with them, but to give them their full meaning"* (Matthew 5:17). Jesus spent his whole life living a Jewish life. He kept the *Kosher* dietary laws. He taught in the synagogue almost every Sabbath. He followed the Jewish Law in circumcision and the practice of Bar Mitzvah. As a Christian, I had been fighting everything that Jesus' life was: A Jewish life.

As part of the conversion to Judaism, the Jewish law requires that one immerse in a *Mikveh*. The experience in the Mikveh is very spiritual ritual, overseen by Rabbi Hornstein, and consists of blessings and reciting the appropriate Jewish prayers while being immersed in a tub that is dedicated for this specific purpose. The tub at Temple Israel is filled with rainwater that is collected on the roof and filtered into the bath.

You must submerge all the way under the water for the immersion to be complete. This ritual is what John the Baptist, a Jew, followed in the immersion of Jesus, according to Jewish tradition. To me, the immersion symbolized a cleansing, and a starting over in my newfound Jewish life and the beginning of turning my life around.

The final step in the process was to have my own Bar Mitzvah, led by Rabbi Arianna Gordon (agordon@temple-israel.org). Many people that come into the Jewish faith later in life will go through the same steps that the young people follow when they become 12 or 13 years old, just like the ceremony I witnessed a few years back.

In my class there were about 30 people, the majority of them women. Young girls were not allowed to participate in a Bat Mitzvah ceremony when they were of age because it was traditionally a beginning to manhood. It's only been in the last 30 years or so that synagogues have offered the opportunity to women.

I need to clarify that the Hebrew language has male and female versions of its words, much like Spanish, French and many others. A *bar* mitzvah is for the male, a *bat* mitzvah is for the female, and a *b'nai* mitzvah is a single group ceremony that combines men and women.

This final lap is a two-year undertaking that includes learning to read and write the
Hebrew language, chanting of the traditional prayers, and the history of the Jewish people. As a class, we celebrated the holidays and festivals, as well as reviewed all the parts of Judaism.

Personally, I found that learning the ritual prayers that are recited during the Friday night Sabbath service were immediately the most helpful and enabled me to fully participate and understand what was going on. I also enjoyed when a Rabbi would visit the class and pick a modern-day topic and compare it to a Biblical passage or event. The talks were always insightful and thought provoking.

During the second year, the primary focus of the class was on chanting an assigned passage in Hebrew from the Torah during the B'nai Mitzvah ceremony. Each person in the class participates in the ceremony that is incorporated into the regularly scheduled worship service. It is customary to invite family and friends to witness this honorary event.

The Hebrew language is a bit complicated and I didn't realize that it has many parts to it. It is read from right to left, (not left to right as in English), the vowel symbols underneath the Hebrew letters dictate the sound of the word and in some cases, depending on which vowel that is used, can change the entire meaning of the word. Writing the Hebrew letters was a challenge as well.

I readily admit I had a hard time learning Hebrew and, unfortunately, drove my teacher's Sheila Waldman Schiffer and Dalia Shaham nuts while I struggled to comprehend what was going on. They tried to make it easier by assigning me the shortest passage, but still I struggled. I worked on it every day for hours. The challenge with reciting Hebrew is two-fold. Saying the word is one thing, but how it is pronounced is equally important. It is chanted in its own melody and done in a form of a song. I eventually came up with my own English version of the words to try to remember them.

All in all, the whole process was just downright amazing and as a bonus, I ended up making some great friends.

The discussions of Bible passages we read in class were not enough. So I started reading the Old Testament (*Tanakh*) on my own. It may surprise a lot of people that the Tanakh is pretty much the same as the Christian version of the Old Testament. Quite frankly, the only differences between the two were simply the order of the books and some very small differences on the meaning of the passages. The Hebrew version of the Old Testament is nice because the English translation is on the left side of the page and the Hebrew is on the right.

Chapter 2

RESHAPING MY VIEW OF MONEY

My first experience with money started at age 12 when I got my first job as a caddie at a local country club. I liked making my own money because I could purchase what I wanted, especially all the things that my parents would not buy me like chocolate bars and ice cream. I remember back in those days my favorite thing to do was to go into a store and buy the biggest chocolate bar I could find.

I worked very hard and earned a lot of money, practically living at the golf course from sun up to sun down. I eventually got promoted to one of the highest rated caddies at the club.

It was also my first initiation into networking as I caddied for a lot of the prominent car dealership owners and local celebrities who turned out to be big tippers. It was my job to carry two large and heavy golf bags but I made double the money and loved doing it.

So by the time I was 16, I had $3000 in the bank. Of course it was a lot of money for a teenager 40 years ago. I had the most money of all the kids I knew and, best of all, I earned it all by myself. I paid cash for a brand new Ford Mustang and was responsible to pay for the gas and up-keep. I enjoyed the money and set a goal to become a millionaire by the time I was 30.

Unfortunately then came the day that my view of money changed abruptly. I started going to a Pentecostal church regularly with my friend Jim Knopp. It is there where I learned that money was evil, that money was no good, that the only people that had money were sinners, and they were going to Hell.

I distinctly remember the story about a man that was denied Heaven because he would not sell all of his possessions and follow Jesus. Even then I knew that your mind would never bring you in a direction that it perceives as wrong so under that influence, I began to think that having money was wrong. Unconsciously I did everything I could to be broke, and that mindset carried on into my adulthood. I would spend all of my money as fast as I earned it.

As I embraced my Jewish faith, I heard that it is good to have money in order to give to others, to provide for your family, and to enjoy your years on this planet with friends. However, I was conflicted, feeling that having money was somehow wrong. It was still ingrained in me that money was evil and it would cause you to go to Hell. Jews do not believe in Hell as a place you go after you die. If you have done something in your life that you regret that may be shameful or wrong, that becomes your Hell on earth. You are able to ask God for forgiveness and repent.

It was during the year of my Introduction to Judaism classes that I discovered a book called "The Secrets of the Millionaire Mind" by T. Harv Eker. (www.harveker.com) I remember stopping sat at a bookstore with the intent of looking for ideas on how to get out of my financial mess. I sat down and started looking through the books that I had picked out. This was odd for me because I hadn't read a book in over 40 years.

Almost immediately, I felt my life changing as I absorbed the message in Eker's book that I was financially broke because of my mindset. His point was that if a person changed their mindset, they can change their life. I read the entire book while at the bookstore and then bought it to re-read at home that night and two more times after that.

I couldn't wait to find out more about *The Millionaire Mind* and began doing some online research. I was thrilled to find out that Eker's leads the *Millionaire Mind Intensive* seminars. This is an organization that holds weekend events around the country. There was one such program coming up a few weeks later in Florida.

At this point in my financial struggle, I was creatively juggling my credit cards balances by switching back and forth between cards with the lowest interest. One of the "new" cards had just given me a higher credit limit and without hesitation, I used the available money to book an airline ticket to Florida and went to the event. Luckily, I was able to stay with a friend while I was there and saved a bunch of money.

The theme of the seminar complimented everything I was learning in my Jewish Journey: that it is okay to have money, that money can do good things for those in need, that money only makes you more of who you are now, and that money is not good or evil but is a tool to unlock your dreams. As I sat there while being so financially broke, this was tough to listen to but it started to shape my mindset to get out of debt and move forward in my life. I was $335,000 in debt and somehow I had hope I could get out of the hole I had dug for myself.

Chapter 3

MONEY IS MORE IMPORTANT THAN ANYONE WILL TELL YOU

A mentor of mine, Dr. Mike Murdock, is an American contemporary Christian singer-songwriter, televangelist and pastor of "The Wisdom Center Ministry" based in Haltom City, Texas. He believes that "money is more important than anyone will ever tell you". Dr. Murdock preaches around the world and is best known for his promotion of a prosperity theology. (www.thewisdomcenter.tv)

When I first listened to him on the Inspiration TV Network (www.insp.com) I thought he was on to something. Money buys food. It enables the means of building hospitals and orphanages. It helps people find shelter. You need money for everything: your transportation, housing, and survival. I will tell you something they don't teach in schools. Money is not either good or evil. Money is just a medium that we use to trade and barter with in order to purchase products and services to live our lives day-to-day.

I learned in my Jewish faith that money is meant to multiply and increase. Money is to be used for good to help others. One's money is meant to carry over to the next generation leaving them better off than the generation before.

I think money is a form of blessing someone or something, because the more money you have, the more blessings you can bestow. The more I embraced my Jewish faith, the message was clear. God loves me and wants me to prosper. He wants me to possess the land and have abundance.

"Bring ye the whole tithe into the store-house, That there may be food in My house. And try Me now herewith. Saith the Lord of Hosts, If I will not open you the windows of heaven, And pour you out a blessing, that there shall be more than sufficiency.   Psalm 50:10

Chapter 4

HONOR YOUR MOTHER AND FATHER: THE FIRST COMMANDMENT WITH A PROMISE

As a Jew, I took great solace and pride in making all of the Ten Commandments an integral part of my life. As a Christian, I was taught that the Ten Commandments were no longer relevant and that the Old Testament was not nearly as important as the New Testament. I was told the Ten could be replaced by two: love thy neighbor as thyself, and the well-known bible verse, referred to as the Golden Rule, "do to others as you would have them do to you".

The one commandment I worked hardest on was honoring my mother and father. It is the first commandment that comes with a promise from God. God promised that by honoring your parents it would go well with you all the days of your life.

Dr. Murdock tells us that our parents are our connection to God. Our parents brought us into this world so it is most important to acknowledge that connection. By honoring them, you are indirectly honoring God.

On the other hand, for some people, respecting their parents can be very challenging. It also makes this the most difficult relationship they can have but it's still the closest and life-shaping relationship in anyone's life. However, no matter the relationship status that you have with them, it has to be a relationship of honor.

I had to make a conscious effort to show my parents honor by never raising my voice to them, and treating them with the highest respect. I also think it's an important to never disrespect your parents, to never talk bad about them, and to never say or do anything condescending toward them.

You should honor your parents at every opportunity you have. One way to honor them is to celebrate their birthdays and anniversaries, simply celebrating them as the most important people in your life. Another way to honor them is with your money. You can take care of the restaurant bill and pay for their meals. I think it's important to make sure that they attain care for the rest of their lives. When they get older, you may need to make sure to provide them with housing if it becomes necessary. It really is the right thing to do.

As part of my effort to honor my parents, in 2009, I sent them a $250 check for Christmas. It was so liberating. It was powerful. It was so stupid because I didn't have $250 in my bank account. I thought I did, but forgot about a check I had sent out for a utility bill and had to wait until my next paycheck to cover the $250. It took me a couple of weeks but I was able to the money to cover the check. I never told them I didn't have the money in the bank until several weeks later. They were in such shock they did not know what to do but eventually did cash the check. Not one of their three kids had ever given them any money. We were all living paycheck to paycheck.

Dr. Murdock believes that it is nearly impossible to have any type of wealth and create a legacy for your children without honoring your parents. I, too, believe that without honoring your parents it is very difficult to succeed.

The majority of people seem to want to do it alone but the effort is a hundred times more difficult. I found that most of the people I know had their parent guide them to who they are today.

But what if you don't have parents who have achieved the kind of success you envision for yourself? What if you don't have supportive parents? What if your parents are deceased?

We all have something that we want to forget from our childhood. As for me, I had several things. I found that through visualization you can rewrite the script in your mind. A technique I used was to visualize a painful situation through the eyes of my parents and realized they did the best they could in many of the situations. In other situations, I found it was easier to rewrite the script and play it back in my mind in a positive outcome. For me, it was important to reimagine the negative experience with a positive outcome.

Another tool I used comes from Dr. Murdock. It's a technique he calls "The Circle of Seven". The key is to surround yourself with seven people of higher prosperity than yourself. Look for people with more experience, greater wisdom, and who you want to emulate. For example, if you want to become a millionaire, your inner circle should include people who have achieved that financial level and above.

When I was forming my Circle of Seven, I chose people who I admired for their greatness and the position they had achieved in their lives. Did I know them when I began the selection process? A few were people I knew, but most I had to seek out to actually meet them, and the rest, I pretended they were in my Circle. The people who I had personal relationships with I would call from time to time and talk over my issue. For the others, I would mentally convene my group around my imaginary round table and ask them how they would handle my issue. I can hear you now! He's kidding, right? Whether or not you choose to include your parents in your inner circle, is of course, optional.

My parents, Ralph and Emily Asp, created a successful business, Doors of Pontiac, located in Waterford, MI in 1977. People often ask, why was it named "Doors of Pontiac" when it's located in the neighboring city of Waterford? When they first opened the business it was actually in the city of Drayton Plains, a tiny area that has since been absorbed by Waterford. It's an area so small that no one ever had heard of it, except the people who lived there. My dad, always thinking bigger, decided the largest city closest to the store was Pontiac, thus the name, Doors of Pontiac.

The tagline, "The Best Little Door House in Michigan", came about after my dad saw Dolly Parton in the movie "Best Little Whorehouse in Texas". Everyone caught the play on words, and it just stuck.

Prior to starting the company, my dad worked in the swimming pool business in the summer months and in the winter, he worked for a door company in Detroit. He found he liked the door business and together with my mom, took a leap of faith and went out on their own opening the little storefront of Doors of Pontiac.

My dad believed that the most important thing was to provide quality service to his customers and he passed that belief on to me. He always upgraded the doors with the best hinges and rollers and always sold the best products available.

I remember it was tough having your parents' start a business. They worked long hours to provide for us and it was not easy. They had to take a second mortgage on the house to start the business and they worked extremely hard to make the business what it is today.

Up until this point, I had blamed my parents for a lot of my unhappiness throughout my life. I kept my distance from my parents. I couldn't understand why they worked so much and were away from home most of the time. Now, of course, I understand if they didn't work as hard as they did, we would have probably lost our house and everything we had.

I'm sure the majority of people will tell you that they resent their parents for one reason or another, or that their childhood didn't measure up to their idea of how it should have been. It's quite an uphill battle for children to grow up in an environment where the parents aren't supportive and the relationships with their children are strained.

I came to grips that the past is the past. I am an adult now and I am responsible for myself. I look back and know that my parents did the best job they knew how and with the tools they had to work with. I consciously chose to honor my father and mother. Honor does not erase the past. Honor does not allow abuse. Honor does not mean everything turns out okay. It just means I honor them for bringing me into this world and bringing me to this point.

I made up with my parents and I love them with all my heart. It is amazing sometimes that I will bring up a bad experience and ask why my dad did this or that. And it's just as amazing to hear his reason for it. It seems he never saw things quite the way I saw it. His perspective was that he was only acting in a way that would straighten me out for doing something wrong and disciplined me because he felt I was doing wrong.

The movie that struck a chord within me was the 2017 film, "The Shack". It is an American Christian drama based on the 2007 novel of the same name by William P. Young. The plot follows the story of Mack Phillips, who after suffering a family tragedy, spirals into a deep depression that causes him to question his innermost beliefs. Facing a crisis of faith, he receives a mysterious letter urging him to visit an abandoned shack in the Oregon wilderness. Despite his doubts, Mack journeys to the shack and encounters a mysterious trio of strangers led by a woman named Papa. Through this meeting, Mack finds important truths that will transform his understanding of his tragedy and change his life forever.

I won't spoil the movie with all the details but the trio of strangers gradually reveal their identities. The purpose of their invitation to visit the shack in the woods was to first help him to better understand his life as seen from a much broader context or higher perspective. This realization helps free him from an inclination to pass judgment upon himself as well as upon everyone else who crosses his path. It is from that new starting point that he may then continue his long, slow journey into healing for himself and his family and forgiveness for himself as well as for those who have grievously harmed him and his loved ones.

Seeing this movie changed my perspective of my relationship with my parents and carried over to many other aspects of my life as well.

Chapter 5

BE A PROFESSIONAL GIVER

When it comes to being a "giver", a Jewish friend of mine, Steve, could not have said it any better. He said from the time he was young, his Mom would always say, "No po and no pig", which translates to mean that you are not supposed to be poor and not to eat pork. She always told him that God wants all of us to prosper and have increase.

My friend went on to explain that the reason most Jews don't eat pork is because pigs are not considered *Kosher*, as they don't digest their food (chew their cud). Kosher foods are those that conform to the Jewish dietary regulations, and the preparation of the food is overseen by a Rabbi. Observant Jews do not eat pork or shellfish and they don't mix dairy foods in the same meal as meat.

My friend told me that God doesn't want us to be poor and that it's actually looked down on amongst our community. You become a taker instead of being a giver. It sounded logical to me.

> *"And I will rebuke the devourer for your good. And he shall not destroy the fruits of your land; neither shall your vine cast its fruit before the time in the field, Saith the Lord of hosts."* (Malachi 3:11)

I always thought of myself as giver but found out that I was not a giver at all. To be truly a giver, one has to give so much it hurts. Why is this important as you embrace the wealth principles?

This expands your focus in giving back to God. I realized it was a way to say to God, "it is all yours anyway. I am just a caretaker."

I believe when looking for an outlet to give your money, you need to specifically look for a ministry or non-profit charity that honors God and targets helping people that have physical, financial, or emotional difficulties. This purposeful giving enables your money to be reaching someone to better their life and overcome their situation that is holding them back from living a prosperous and fulfilling life. They need to see God's goodness as a result of your giving.

My first lesson in giving happened on a night when I was in bed watching the television. Televangelist Dr. Mike Murdock was presenting an engaging talk on how God can break the back of personal poverty when the viewer sends his ministry $1,000. He even went so far as to say "if you don't have the money readily available, consider putting on your credit card".

Well, that sure got my full attention. I said to myself, this is the stupidest, most obnoxious thing I ever heard of in my life. I thought, there is no way I could believe a guy that says he is a man of God yet could fleece the flock and take their hard-earned money.

I listened as Dr. Murdock told how he grew up in poverty. As an adult, he went through a divorce and of course, that threw him even deeper in debt. He had no furniture, no window shades, no nice clothes to wear and had no money for food. I could certainly relate.

He said his inspiration to change came after he attended a seminar presented by Pentecostal Evangelist Charles Greenaway, who told Dr. Murdock that if he wanted to increase his wealth, he needed to "expand the corners of his field". It is an Old Testament concept from the book of Ruth.

In the Old Testament, the rich were instructed to leave the corners of their barley or wheat fields for the poor. God told them that "Your field is your income. Your corners represent your outgo to God. If you will increase the size of your corners, God will increase the size of your field, or your income."

In the story, Ruth was destitute so she took to gathering excess food from a land owner named Boaz. When Boaz left the food around the corners of his property to feed the poor, his wealth increased. I was surprised to discover that Ruth was the first convert to Judaism in the Bible.

> *"When you reap the harvest of your land, you shall not reap all the way to the corner of your field, or gather the gleanings of your harvest. You shall not pick your vineyard bare, or gather the fallen fruit of your vineyard; you shall leave them for the poor and the stranger; I the Lord am your God".* (Leviticus 19:9-11)

Dr. Murdock continued to say that when you give, it doesn't leave your life, it's an investment into your future. As I'm listening to him speak, I begin to mentally review my situation and how similar it was to Murdock's past. I was desperate and broke to the point of having sleepless nights. I kept switching credit cards to any company that would allow me to transfer my balances and keep the 0% interest that I had maintained. I knew that I was running out of time until no one would let me continue to transfer.

I was so desperate that I wanted to believe his stories of how he broke the back of poverty and through his giving, it came back to him a hundredfold. He went on to say that in the story of Malachi, God asks his people to test him and to give. Then, if in giving it comes back to you in the form of blessings and favors, this is your proof that God exists. Dr. Murdock said this is the only place in Bible where God says to put Him to a test. I read that verse back and forth and thought, "why not? I will try it".

> *"Bring ye the whole tithe into the storehouse. That there may be food in MY house. And try me now herewith. Saith the Lord of Hosts, If I will not open you the windows of heaven, And pour you out a blessing, That there shall be more than sufficiency".* (Malachi 3:10)

At that moment it occurred to me that I had just transferred my credit card balance to a company that had increased my credit limit and surprisingly, I had just over $1,000 available until I maxed the card out. I figured at this point, what did I to lose? I couldn't pay off the credit card in 10 years, so what's an extra year? So without hesitation, I called the TV station and put $1,000 on my credit card.

I know what you're thinking. If you were living paycheck-to-paycheck, not making ends meet, why would you do that? I think the only explanation I can give was that I was so desperate and was just hoping by faith that this would work. I told myself when you are $335,000 in debt with just $.57 in your savings account, another $1,000 will not make any difference.

I paid the credit card off within 45 days with a completely unexpected tax refund of $24,000. That has never happened to me before and hasn't happened since. I immediately sent another $1,000 to the ministry. The blessings have never stopped and my giving to Dr. Murdock's ministry has increased every year since. For me, it changed my life. I've had one blessing after another and my giving continued to increase.

Dr. Murdock was adamant that God wants us to give. I'd been wrestling with that whole notion, all the while wondering what was the big deal about giving. He explained that the reason that God gets upset when we don't give is because he cannot bless us if we don't. So it is really an interesting concept.

In Deuteronomy 1:11, it is written, *"The Lord, the God of your fathers, make you a thousand times so many more as ye are, and bless you, as He hath promised you!"* In this verse, the Lord, the God of your fathers, gives his promise of favor and blessing. God wants to favor and bless his people, period.

I found it is important to give and to give in "good ground" to get a return. The term *to give in good ground* is a biblical term that translates in modern language to mean that you have to be selective with whom you *give* your time, energy, and attention. You need to seek out like-minded people or people who are on a higher station in life to better yourself. In other words, God has given you a gift that will flourish and grow in *good soil*.

I believe every check is an offering when given to an organization or ministry that does the work of God. So you first must be aware of where you give your money rather than how much you give. God wants to show us favor and blessings but we restrict the flow by not giving back to those who help others. It helps when you direct your offering to a specific destination. I actually note on the lower left corner of every check where I want to see my favor and blessing.

I first started writing on my checks what I wanted to pay off. When you have $335k in debt you have a lot to choose from. I started with a small debt to give me confidence and get them out of the way. I graduated to the bigger debt like my two mortgages, student loans, and my car. Did it work? Yes, it sure did. I even indicated on the checks that I sent to the vendors that I wanted to be debt free, all in correlation to what I wanted to accomplish at that time.

Another way to give is sacrificially. I don't believe tithing is a New Testament concept at all. I always thought it was a funny thing that the only carryover from the Old Testament that I was ever taught to keep was tithing.

I think it is too bad that churches do not embrace a more Jewish way of life. I rarely hear anything spoken in churches from the Old Testament other than messages about tithing. They miss out on so much of what God is trying to tell them. They miss out on the blessings and favor God wants to give them through the different festivals and in increase thinking.

So along my Jewish journey I learned that favor and blessing, as well as giving, go hand-in-hand. A great example of giving can be seen in the story of King Solomon:

> *"And the king went to Gibeon to sacrifice there: for that was the great high place: a thousand burnt-offerings did Solomon offer upon the alter." (*1 Kings 3:4)
>
> *"and Solomon offered for the sacrifice of peace-offerings, which he offered unto the Lord, two and twenty thousand oxen and a hundred and twenty thousand sheep. So the king and all the children of Israel dedicated the house of the Lord." (*1 Kings 8:13)

The reason that Solomon had such great wealth is because he gave these offerings. In addition, he celebrated the Jewish festivals and holidays. Did you notice that the first act of giving Solomon gave was for a 1,000 burnt offerings? Later, it was an offering of 120,000 sheep and 22,000 oxen. The point is it is all about giving and, in return, getting increase, and with that increase, you can turn around and you can give more. It's a never-ending cycle. Look for people and organizations to give to and I believe God will bless you accordingly.

A more modern way of giving is to give to others. My wife, Donna, and I set up a fund to help others. I remember how I felt not having money to go my daughter's graduation and knew I wasn't alone. During my journey, I have met many people, through no fault of their own, who have fallen into hard times. We set up the fund at Temple Israel to help people within the community who are in need of emergency assistance. The "Donna and Alan Emergency Assistance Fund", is set up much like Dr. Murdock's ministry, to receive seed donations to help others. If you would like to send a donation, it can be sent to Temple Israel, 5725 Walnut Lake Rd, West Bloomfield Township, MI 48323. Your check can be made out to the Donna and Alan Emergency Assistance fund. All proceeds from the sale of this book will be donated to this fund.

Chapter 6

LIVING WITHIN YOUR MEANS

Living within your means is a lesson I lived and learned the hard way. Most people don't seem to understand the concept because it's against the American way of thinking. In order to live within your means you can't spend your hard earned money on things you can't afford. Sounds simple enough, right?

T. Harv Eker, author of the Millionaire Mind, uses a method of budgeting that he calls "The Jars Method of Living". Under this budgeting system, I was able to get my finances under control.

The Jars Method suggests living on 50% of your income. The remaining money is distributed this way: 10% goes toward giving, 10% is in an untouchable retirement account, 10% you use to educate and expand yourself, 10% gets set aside for long-term goals, and the last 10% is your fun money.

When I examined my own budget, I quickly came to terms that my life was in complete shambles. I was living on 100% my income and spending 30% on fun. I was giving 0%. I was giving 0% back to myself. I was spending 0% educate and expand myself. I was saving 0% for long-term growth. I was living above my means and spending more than I made. I was traveling way too much, serial dating, going out to eat for every meal, and spending like there was no end to the money. If you can relate, the good news is that you can change, just as I did.

My new budget looked like this: $600 per week was broken into the six "jars". I lived on 50% ($300), I gave 10% ($60), my play money was 10% ($60), 10% went toward paying down the debt

($60), 10% went to education, seminars and books ($60), and the last 10% went into the never-spend long-term investments jar ($60). Quite a difference in my spending habits.

I went to the bank and opened five separate bank accounts. My child support came off the top and was sent out first. The remainder of my paycheck was direct deposited into one account and had 10% taken out automatically for the 401(K) long term account. The remaining money was moved to the other accounts. It wasn't until I got my finances in order that began to feel the chaos melt away and felt in balance with God and the Universe.

Chapter 7

HONOR GOD
BE AT PEACE WITH GOD

My faith journey started when I went to the seminary in 1979 to fulfill my religious training, and then continued my studies at a religious college. This training prepared me to become an Assembly of God minister for the next ten years. I served in roughly ten churches and have been a type of pastor in five different Assembly of God churches. I thought I knew the Bible inside and out. I was called on to deliver over 1,000 sermons, preaching around the United States, yet somehow, deep down in my soul I always felt that something was missing.

I originally thought I had followed my Christian path out of duty as well as at God's will and direction for my life but eventually this just became a job to me. It still was a form of honor to God but I guess in a sense, I just didn't understand the concept of true honor.

It was during my initial visit to Temple Israel that I realized that I actually in fact had no relationship with God. This may be a bit hard to understand, but in the Christian world people refer to God as God, Jesus as God, and The Holy Spirit as God, or commonly known as The Trinity, which is one God living in three Divine Persons. I most certainly did not feel a direct connection with God himself.

I was determined to learn and know about my father God and this became the driving force of my Jewish Journey. I know it sounds odd to some but the only way I can explain it is to think of growing up with only one parent. I had no idea who my father God was and it made me so unhappy and unfulfilled, and most certainly, I was not at peace with myself. I think back to a scripture, *"The confident mind you guard in safety. In safety because it trusts in you"*. (Isaiah 26:3)

In developing my relationship with God, I found that the number one thing to do is simply honor God. There are so many ways to do that. One way you can honor God this through giving of your time and money. Another way is by doing religious service. You can help others in need. You can pray. And as we have already discussed, you honor God by observing the Sabbath, festivals and holidays.

When I began attending the services, especially the weekly Sabbath services, I discovered that every part of the service is dedicated to honoring God. Just after sundown on Friday nights, each service begins with the lighting of candles, the traditional blessings and upbeat songs that signify the beginning of Shabbat. The format of the service hasn't changed much in the last 5,778 years of the Jewish history. Of course, the tone of the services have been adopted to more modern times. It's only been in the last 30 years that women have been readily welcomed to join the service and over the last two decades, they often include a choir, musical accompaniment, and digital screen projections.

The middle portion of the service is the reciting of the ritual prayers including the watchword of the Jewish faith, the *Shema,* and the *Kaddish*, the prayer for the departed loved ones. The service winds down with a topical sermon by the rabbi, and ends with a song of friendship, with congregants holding hands or swaying and embracing each other. Immediately, after the service, everyone gathers at a reception that celebrates the fellowship and, my favorite, the over-the-top pastries and coffee.

As I mentioned earlier, Jews honor God by reading and speaking the prayers in Hebrew because that's the only language God gave to man. Another way that the men show honor to God is to wear the traditional skull-cap, a head covering called a *Yamaka* or a *Kippah,* and a prayer shawl, called a *Tallis*. In the reform synagogues, like the one I belong to, it is not as important that you wear a *Kippah* or *Tallis* but most men do out of respect. Generally, it is only married women who wear head coverings such as hats or scarves in synagogue, but the more religious women will wear wigs or head coverings at all times and out in public as well.

When a Jew chooses to observe the Sabbath from sundown on Friday night to sundown on Saturday night, it becomes a 24-hour period of rest and renewal as well as family time.

> *"By the seventh day God had finished the work he had been doing; so on the seventh day he rested from all his work. And God blessed the seventh day and made it holy, because on it he rested from all the work of creating that he had done"* (Genesis 2:2, 3).

As I've said before, I think a very important way to honor God is to keep the Festivals and Holidays and to celebrate them with my community. In my past, I could never understand when I heard that Jesus kept all the festivals. Perhaps he was supposed to be a guide for the Christian faith but as a Christian, I never kept any of the festivals. I think if you were to follow what Jesus set forth as an example, the Three Pilgrimage Festivals and the High Holy Days are most important.

Passover, the first of the Three Pilgrimage Festivals, is my personal favorite of the festivals, and is the celebration of how the Israelites were liberated from slavery in Egypt. I can just imagine how Jesus as a Jew felt observing the Passover Seder with the 12 Jewish Disciples remembering the great miracle God performed and how they praised God for that amazing event. The Passover Seder coincides with the Last Supper Jesus had before the Crucifixion.

Passover is celebrated over eight days in the early spring. The first two nights of the holiday feature a *Sedar*, a special ceremonial meal built around items symbolizing the bitterness and harshness of the slavery which the Jews endured in ancient Egypt. Throughout the holiday, Jews eat *matzah*, or unleavened bread, to commemorate that the Israelites left in such haste they didn't have time to let the yeast rise in order to bake bread. The meals prepared during this holiday do not include bread or any leavening and most people observe the Kosher-style of eating.

A great telling of the story of Exodus is in watching the 1956 movie, "The Ten Commandments", that depicts the narrative of the Exodus, led by Moses, (Charlton Heston in the movie) and tells how God inflicted the ten plagues on the Egyptians before the Pharaoh would release the slaves. The tenth and worst of the plagues being the death of the Egyptian first born sons.

The Israelites were instructed by Moses to mark the doorposts of their homes with the blood of a slaughtered spring lamb and, upon seeing this mark, the spirit of the Lord knew to pass over the first-born in these homes. That is how the holiday got its name.

The Israelites made it across the desert to the Red Sea and were trapped as the Pharaoh (who had a change of heart) and his army chased after them to bring them back to slavery. But God parted the Red Sea, allowing the Israelites to cross safely. When the Egyptians followed into the sea, the water came crashing down on them, and wiped out the army.

An interesting part of the story is that the Red Sea only parted when Nachshon, the brother-in-law of Aaron, stepped into the water. This is important to point out because God only responds when we step out in faith.

The Israelites then wandered in the desert for 40 years before reaching the Promised Land of Israel.

As I started to explore my Jewish faith, I traveled to Israel and saw it for myself. I had the privilege to go to the traditional place where the crossing of the Red Sea took place. It is a place off the coast of Egypt and stretches to the coast of Saudi Arabia. My friend, Jeff Settle, and I leased out a large boat and went out into the

Red Sea to where the Israelites crossed. We did do some fishing along the way and from the southern tip of Israel, where we entered the Red Sea, you can literally see the borders of Jordan, Saudi Arabia and Egypt. They can't be more than several miles apart. According to a local tour guide, there are still chariot wheels at the bottom of the Red Sea.

I saw the sites. I went to where it all began. I saw the lands of "milk and honey'. I saw where the Temple once stood. I walked the ancient streets of old city. I went to Massada and to the Western Wall. I met the people and found that they were people, just like me, who wanted to live a life in peace and safety.

The Feast of Pentecost, also known as *Shavout*, is the second of the Three Pilgrimage Festivals and occurs on the sixth day of the Hebrew month of Sivan (between mid-May and mid-June). It commemorates the anniversary of the day God gave the Torah to the entire nation of Israel assembled at Mount Sinai. It also marks the wheat harvest in the Land of Israel.

The word *shavuot* means "weeks", and the festival marks the completion of the seven-week of the *Counting of the Omer*, a period that begins on the second day of Passover, and is understood to express anticipation and desire for the giving of the Torah to the Israelite.

The Feast of Tabernacles, or *Sukkot*, is the third of the Three Pilgrimage Festivals on which the Israelites were commanded to perform a pilgrimage to the Temple in Jerusalem. The holiday is celebrated on the fifteenth day of the seventh month on the Hebrew calendar and varies from late September to late October. It is observed five days after the High Holy Day of Yom Kippur, the Day of Atonement, the most sacred of the Jewish holidays.

Sukkot lasts seven days in Israel and eight days everywhere else. It has an agricultural significance and marks the end of the harvest time in Israel. The more biblical significance to the holiday is found in the Book of Leviticus and commemorates the Exodus and the dependence of the People of Israel on the will of God.

The Hebrew word *sukkot* means "tabernacle" or "booth". During the holiday, it is customary to build a walled structure covered with plant material such as palm leaves, as stated in Leviticus, and is reminiscent of the type of fragile dwellings in which the Israelites lived in during their 40 years of travel in the desert after their Exodus from slavery in Egypt. Throughout the holiday, meals are eaten inside the sukkah and many people sleep in there as well.

The holiest of holidays that Jews observe are *Rosh Hashanah* and *Yom Kippur*. Rosh Hashanah is the Jewish New Year and literally means the "beginning of the year". It is the first of the High Holy Days that usually occur in the early autumn. It is a two-day holiday which begins on the first day of *Tishrei*, the first month of the Jewish new year and marks the start of the ten days of atonement. It is also the traditional anniversary of the creation of Adam and Eve, and their inauguration of humanity's role in God's world.

The customs include sounding the *shofar,* a hollowed-out ram's horn, reciting special liturgy and enjoying festive meals. It is customary to eat symbolic foods such as apples dipped in honey that signifies the wish for a "sweet new year".

Yom Kippur, also known as the Day of Atonement, is the holiest day of the year in Judaism, and is traditionally observed with 24-hours of fasting and intensive prayer, with people often spending most of the day in the synagogue. According to Jewish tradition, God inscribes each person's fate for the coming year into the Book of Life on Rosh Hashanah and waits until Yom Kippur to "seal" the verdict. During the Days of Awe (the period between the two holidays), a Jew tries to amend his or her behavior and seek forgiveness for wrongs done against God and against other human beings. The evening before and day of Yom Kippur are set aside for public and private petitions and confessions of guilt. At the end of Yom Kippur, one hopes that they have been forgiven by God.

Chapter 8

BE A PROFESSIONAL LEARNER

Throughout the course of my Christian college studies, my impression of the Old Testament was that it was about documenting wars, violence, do's and don't's, and stories that would never be practical or prevalent in my life. However, early on in my Jewish journey, I decided to re-read all 39 books of the Old Testament, from Genesis to Malachi, but this time, through new eyes. This is when I began to notice that the wealth principles were right there. And that's when I decided to be "a life-long learner".

I had heard that if someone asked Dr. Mike Murdock what his profession is, he would always say, "I am a life-long learner". For the longest time I couldn't consider myself a learner at all. It seems crazy now looking back but from ages 22 to 47, I hadn't read a single book. I thought my lack of reading was nuts until I talked to a friend who told me that it's pretty common since most of the book sales in the world are purchased in other countries. I looked it up. It's a documented fact that most males in the United States do not read at all. I took a poll amongst my male friends and asked them when was the last time they had read a book, cover to cover. The answer was unanimously, "I don't remember".

The bottom line is simply this: if you want to expand your mind, you need to read. With an infinite number of books to choose from, start with reading books that will enable you to become an expert in whatever is your passion. God made us all different and each one of us has something unique to give back to God and the Universe. You need to discover your passion, your purpose in life.

When you find your passion, you can turn that passion into making money.

Have you ever watched the reality television program "Shark Tank"? Budding entrepreneurs get a chance to "pitch" their ideas to the five titan "sharks in the tank" with the hope that they will invest their own money into the contestant's product or service. The contestants have invested their own money, and in most cases, have mortgaged their homes, and heavily borrowed money from friends and family, all in the hopes of getting their product in the marketplace. The billionaire sharks have already made their own dreams a reality and turned their own ideas into lucrative empires. The fun is when more than one of the sharks decides they want a piece of the action, a bidding war can erupt, and that drives up the price of the investment. Or sometimes, the Sharks just offer constructive criticism, and all of them pass on the opportunity to invest. What is the most interesting to me about watching the show, and I've watched it well over 100 times, is that the Shark's will never put their own money into something they are not passionate about because they know it will never succeed. They want not only to get their money back but to make a huge profit on the investment as well.

We are all different people with very diverse interests but when you find your passion or purpose, you need to become an expert and learn everything you can about the about it. If you are in the flower business, for example, and that is your passion, you can read everything you can get your hands on about flowers and starting a floral business. It won't take long before you could know more than your boss and go out on your own, starting your own floral business.

Oh sure, when will I find the time to do that, you ask? Instead of turning on the television every night when you go home, you could use that time to read. Do you spend a lot of time driving from here to there during the day? You can pop in a CD or tape instead of listening to the radio. Pick any topic that will add to your education, be it biographies of someone you admire and aspire to emulate, or self-help audio books to better yourself.

Another way to benefit from what others have learned about the area you want to explore, YouTube (www.youtube.com) is filled with videos made by experts. Simply enter your subject in the search bar and I'll bet hundreds of videos appear for your viewing pleasure.

No matter if it's books, CD's or videos, you need to continually educate yourself and become the best you can be. You can personally seek out other experts in your chosen field and ask them questions about whatever subject you are trying to find out about. Their expertise is learned the hard way and can help you see things from a different perspective, saving you time and energy in your quest to become an expert and improve yourself. Learn what others do not know. Expand your mind and you will expand your future.

I've noticed that anybody and everybody that has made something of themselves, when they were broke and desperate, all decided to read every book they could on the subject that they most wanted to learn and improve on, i.e. how to make more money. Two good examples of people who educated themselves and expanded by reading books are Tai Lopez, and Grant Cardone. Lopez is a consultant and coach who teaches his theory of living a healthy, wealthy, and happy life, and went from destitute to owning over 20 multi-million dollar businesses. (www.tailopez.com) Cardone was destitute but went on to create a multi-million dollar empire as a top sales trainer and social media personality. (www.grantcardone.com)

You need to find out about the people that went before you. Find out how they became an expert because they are the piece to the puzzle to increase your wealth. A few of my favorite books are: "The Millionaire Mind" by T. Harv Eker, "Think and Grow Rich" by Napoleon Hill, "The Millionaire Next Door" by Thomas J. Stanley and William P. Danko and of course, "The Wisdom Journal" by Dr. Mike Murdock. I find that when you have many books at your disposal, you have more intelligence and confidence.

When I started the process I had zero books and now I have over 500 and I aim to read a book a week, 52 books a year.

I like to buy books and CD's on Amazon, sometimes for as little as a penny. Also I combine book buying and donating to a worthy organization by shopping at local library book sales. Most libraries have them quarterly throughout the year.

Personally, I have collected every book that I can find on stocks and options. Why? Not only do I read them to pursue my passion and expand my mind, I turned the information I learned into making me an expert trader. I've developed my own style and system that I teach to my clients. Trading is one of the money-making ventures I developed to propel me to financial freedom, and leaving a legacy for my children.

In the Millionaire Mind Intensive course, author T. Harv Eker defines "financial freedom" as the "ability to live the lifestyle you desire without having to work or rely on anyone else for money. I worked out of necessity not by choice. After taking the leap into trading as a secondary money stream or "passive income", I grew beyond my weekly paycheck. Passive income is income resulting from cash flow received on a regular basis, requiring minimal to no effort by the recipient to maintain it. The difference between working income and passive income, is that you have to work for the working income. According to Eker's, "you become financially free when your passive income exceeds your lifestyle expenses. The trick is to find your method of passive income that will enable you to work because you want to not because you have to.

Chapter 9

SPEAK TO YOUR FUTURE

Are you one of those people who keep revisiting the past? We as humans always go backward, not forward, in our thinking. We want to have excuses when and if we fail. But doesn't it make sense that you can never move forward in your life if you are stuck in your past? As you focus on the future you want to have, you need to come to terms with your past. The past is past, you can't do anything to change what was. In other words, to get to your future, you must not let your past weigh you down. Strive to be the person you want to become from this moment on.

One of my coach's, Forbes Riley (www.forbesfactor.com) likes to ask, what is the earliest memory you have? The reason she asks this question is because when something traumatic happens, many of us will live at that same spot in life. They can never get past it.

As you look toward your future, I believe that you need to write down your goals, perhaps in a journal. You should write down your goals for every year of your life until you are 120 years old. Yes, I said 120 years old! Why? You need to give your mind a destination. When you don't plan ahead, and you think your life is going to stay the way it is, it will. You need to think that life is going to be the way you want it to be.

The easiest way to begin designing your future is by asking yourself "what will my life look like this time next year? Write down these goals in your journal and keep visualizing how your life will look in five years from now, ten years, twenty-years and so on.

After you discover where you want to be, the next step is to set daily goals. Every day, I write 10 things I want to accomplish that day and most of these goals are keeping me pointed in the direction of the future I will create. You need to keep challenging yourself to expand and bring increase into your life. Make sure the goals you set are attainable and manageable. However, if you do not accomplish all the goals for that day, simply continue work on them the next day.

Once you plan out your goals, you need to create a "vision board" of what you want your future to look like. You can take your plan and map how that future will look down to the very smallest of detail. Begin by taking a few deep cleansing breathes and clear your mind and focus on your future plans. Write it all down in your journal, being very specific on what you want.

What does your house look like? Is your furniture contemporary or mid-century style? Is there a pool in the backyard? What shape is it? Do you have a patio or a lenai? How is it landscaped? What kind of car is parked in the driveway? What color is it? Your life can be created by you, starting with your imagination.

When you get that exact picture in your mind, you need to put it in front of you by creating an actual illustration of your dreams. The vision board can take any form you want. I've seen them on all sizes of poster board, a cork-style bulletin board, or just a plain 8x10 sheet of paper. I, of course, went big, using four full walls in a spare bedroom. I must have had over 1,000 push-pin holes in the wall when I was done.

You begin by cutting pictures or phrases out of magazines or downloading images from the internet that illustrate everything you want to accomplish or own in your life. Visualize that new house, the new car, the perfect job, the places you want to travel to, describe the relationship you yearn for, or anything your heart desires. By creating these vision boards, we give our mind a target to focus on as we attract these things into our future.

When you wake up every morning, you need to start your day with positive thoughts that are warm, calm and encouraging. It helps to create affirmations that reflect your dreams and desires. This is a tool that the Millionaire Mind uses. These affirmations change your mindset and encourage you to focus on how you shape your future. This practice will set the tone for your entire day. When you think and dream with a positive attitude with your future in mind, it doesn't leave room for you to dwell on the past.

I believe your thoughts are more important than you might believe and, to quote the founder of Mary Kay Cosmetics, Mary Kay Ash, "what you perceive you can achieve".

A valuable tool I used when I had $.57 in my savings account was to write checks out for everything I wanted for the rest of my life. I wrote checks to cover the trips I wanted to take, the car I wanted to drive, and the house I wanted to buy, etc. It was a novel idea but one that worked really well for me because a lot of the checks I wrote for these things, I was able to cash.

Since you have mapped out your goals it will be easy to write the checks for your future. Truthfully, I don't know where I got this idea but it probably changed my life more than anything else I tried. You take an actual checkbook from a bank account you currently have and you write out a dated check for everything you desire and the date you want it to occur. Start out with a check written for $100 and increase by $100 increments. Then you jump to $2,000 and increase the checks by $1,000 increments and so on up to $1 million. Keep writing checks after $1 million increasing by $5 million increments. After $10 million, you can write your checks by $10 million increments to $1 billion. Does it work? When I had $.57 in my savings account and I filled out checks for $5,000, $10,000, $20,000, $50,000, $100,000, $200,000 and $1 million, was I able to cash them in my future? Yes I sure did.

This exercise is so powerful because it's an act of faith. It's not your job to figure out when those checks will be able to be cashed. That's where faith comes into play.

I wrote out checks for the pool I wanted, the car I wanted, and the house with the pool I wanted. I wrote checks for the furniture and carpet for the house. I even wrote a check to the guy I hired to paint the house. You need to think of all the specific details then you write your dreams on four checks. This exercise enables your mind to expand even more and is probably the greatest goal setting tool I used in my financial recovery.

I believe people never acquire what they desire because they don't give it serious thought and never put it down on paper, let alone never go so far as write a check, even if the money isn't available quite yet for what they want. It's not our job to figure out how or when the money will be deposited in the account. Our job is to just have faith that it will materialize.

Actor and comedian Jim Carrey grew up impoverished and got his start as a stand-up comic at 15 years old. In his debut performance at a Toronto comedy club he bombed so badly that he questioned whether he could make a living as an entertainer. As you can see, he didn't give up. The next year he dropped out of high school to pursue his career.

At 19, Carrey headed to Hollywood but like many young actors looking for their big break, he found that success was elusive. In 1985, broke and depressed, Carrey drove his old, beat-up Toyota up the Hollywood hills and sitting overlooking Los Angeles, he daydreamed of success. He wrote himself a check for $10 million for "acting services rendered", post-dated it 10 years and kept the check in his wallet.

The check remained in his wallet until it deteriorated. Carrey, of course, eventually made it in Hollywood and earned millions of dollars starring in movies like *Ace Ventura: Pet Detective, The Mask,* and *Dumb and Dumber.* When his father passed away in 1994, Carrey slipped the check into the casket to be buried with him.

In 1878, Thomas Edison tried to figure out the light bulb. He was not the inventor of the light bulb; 20 other people created it before him. He wanted to perfect it and make it so it worked for a long period of time combined with electricity. He tried over 1,000 times and finally gave up. He went to bed and asked the Universe to help him. He took a nap and in a dream, he solved the mystery of electricity and the light bulb. In his dream he saw that a light bulb will work for a long time if it is not exposed to oxygen and he was able to figure out a way to build it. To this day, Thomas Edison if known for creating the light bulb.

Like Carrey and Edison, always dream, and if you are dreaming, dream big.

Chapter 10

BE A MASTER NETWORKER

According to the Merriam-Webster dictionary definition, "networking" is the exchange of information or services among individuals, groups, or institutions; specifically, the cultivation of productive relationships for employment or business". What does that mean?

Social media is just one form of networking. The more popular online networking sites are Facebook, LinkedIn, and Twitter but depending on your age, you may prefer Instagram, Snapchat or have your own personal favorite sites.

Personally, I prefer using Facebook. For the longest time I was happy to have five friends following me on my page. I was an introvert and actually liked to keep to myself. But I have come to realize that you can't stay in your comfort zone if you want to expand your life. I made a conscious effort to start connecting with family, friends and business associates on Facebook, and quickly built my "friends" to 2,610 connections. These people follow me and will notice when I post things of interest about my personal life and business adventures as well. I invite you to follow me at https://www.facebook.com/allan.asp.7 and follow the money trading group. Some people prefer to keep their personal page and business page separate and post their content accordingly.

One thing you need to know about using social media is that it's only as good as the time commitment you plan to devote to posting and marketing your business as well as yourself. If you only have time to post a couple times a week on your Facebook page, that is your choice. You would probably want to skip using Twitter and other time consuming sites. I do recommend, at the very least, that you create a LinkedIn profile as your online resume. Again, the more connections you have, the more noticed you become among those who are searching for someone in your industry. One of the features on LinkedIn is a "wall" similar to Facebook where you can post business related items for all to see. But again, if you are pressed for time, pick one favorite site and stick to that.

In addition to social media, you need to make the effort to physically get out into your world and show your worth to others, especially in your business endeavors. A smart starting point on identifying the most efficient use of your time, energy and money, is to identify who is a good customer for your business.

There are a tremendous amount of entry level networking events available: your local Chamber of Commerce is a good place to start. If anyone can buy your product or service, such as an insurance agent, this is good way to meet people in general. But in most cases, at this entry level, you won't necessarily meet the decision makers of the companies you might wish to target.

However, if you are looking to upgrade your station in life and pick out people who are at a higher level than you, or your product or service is targeted to a specific industry, I suggest a more advance method of networking. You need to seek out the decision makers such as the business owners and community leaders, the ones that you won't find at the entry-level networking events.

One way to meet new people is to volunteer your time with just one of a myriad of organizations such as the Boys and Girls Club or Kiwanis as well as with your church or synagogue. Every two years there is some kind of an election. Pick a cause or a candidate then volunteer to work on that campaign. You are guaranteed to meet community leaders and business owners you wouldn't ordinarily meet in your day-to-day activities.

A friend who has spent years in public relations suggests that you attend opportunities at your local country clubs, yacht clubs, and other private organizations where the community leaders frequent. Another way to meet the influencers is to attend charity galas and other community fundraisers. You don't always need to be a member of the organization to go to their events and it is another way for you to be a giver. Sometimes the clubs have special events that are open to the public in the hopes that they attract new members. Or you can go through your list of contacts and find out who you know that belongs to a country club or golf club. Why not reach out and ask them to invite you to attend an event as their guest?

My PR friend is adamant that for this more advanced networking, your goal is not to sell anything at your first meeting. She has an 80-20 rule and lets the new contact do 80% of the talking while keeping 20% of the conversation about herself. She is able to ask questions that will help her discover how she can do business with this person, what they have in common or if she knows someone who she can refer this person to do business with as well. At that point, they usually exchange business cards. When my friend walks away, she quickly writes on the back of the card what event they met at and some keywords that will help her remember their conversation.

If she wants to continue a relationship with the new contact, i.e. wants to sell them a product or service, a follow-up email or note suggests they meet for coffee or lunch. Another way she reconnects is to let this person know of an event they might like to attend or if she has someone she'd like to introduce them to.

What do you do with all the business cards you will accumulate after a few of these events? You build a database, of course. You can use your cellphone or create an Excel spreadsheet or use a CRM (customer relationship manager) program on your computer. You can use this contact information to invite people to connect on your social media, to send a newsletter or business flyer, or to invite them to an event such as my book launch party, and so many other applications.

As part of your marketing material, do you have your own website? It's a detailed online business card and creatively lets the world know what your business is all about. You can create your own website through lots of websites, Wix.com, Domain.com, or GoDaddy.com and others. You will need to be sure that your "domain name" is available (the name you want for your website) and you do that by searching the internet for that information. You will also need to subscribe to a hosting service, such as Go Daddy or other hosting company, and that usually is done on a yearly basis.

I suggest getting advice from your favorite computer geek who creates websites for a living. It's worth the investment in letting an expert set up your website. However, after it is up and active, be sure you have access to the site so you can make the necessary changes yourself and/or after the site is created, you are the owner of it, not the guy who created the site.

The whole point of social media and having an online presence is to expand your circle of "friends" and in turn, you will expand your circle of influence. You need to keep expanding in every way you can so as not to be stuck and stagnant in your personal or business life. I had to push myself to make a very conscious effort to get out and network. But the pay-off was all the people I met not only to do business with but also who I wanted to keep as real friends and associates in my new future.

I got my start networking at as a teenager working as a caddie at the local country club without even realizing at the time that I was building relationships with people who could influence my life. Of course, now as a master networker, I purposefully seek out influencers who speak to my future and keep me moving forward.

How did I meet those people who may appear to be out of my range? I seek out mentors who have a proven track record. My first mentor was Mike Williams (www.mikewilliamssolutions.com). He is a marketing consultant who combines marketing and organizational strategies to produce dynamic results for his clients. One of his most notable clients is motivational speaker Les Brown.

    I had seen a motivational CD by Brown and realized we had a lot in common. Brown grew up poor and turned it around. I loved his story and his message. I knew I needed help. So I sought his coach, Mike Williams. I filled out the application on his website and he responded. I was able to work with Williams for over a year and a half. Of course, this coaching also came with a price but it was worth every penny as he fine-tuned the direction I needed to go in my business and personal life.

    I was able to join a weekly conference call with my coach Forbes Riley (www.forbesfactor.com) and during the call the participants could ask her questions about any problem they were having. Her responses were generally of benefit to everyone on the call.

    Some of the other coaches I have used are Oliver Velez, an expert on trading in financial markets (www.olivervelez.com), increase coach Bob Harrison (www.increase.org) confidence coach Dr. Keith Johnson, (www.keithjohnson.tv) and world-renowned trader and trainer, Courtney Smith (www.courtneysmith.com)

    If you aren't able to hire a coach such as these people, YouTube is good source for viewing their motivational talks.

Chapter 11

LIVE TO EAT HEALTHY

I believe it is very important to eat healthy and eat green. I have two favorite books on this subject. The first one is "The Prevent and Reverse Heart Disease Cookbook" by Ann Crile Esselstyn and Jane Esselstyn, and the second book is "How Not to Die" by Michael Greger MD. Following the advice in these books, and eating a plant based lifestyle changed my life.

For 50 years I ate all the wrong foods. I ate a lot of fast food. I ate a lot of processed foods. I ate ice cream, cheese, milk, and meat. What I learned in these books is that we are consuming a lot more than that when we eat or drink the items that I listed. I again do not think these items are all that bad if they could be done in a way to not have all the preservatives and chemicals to make them last for weeks, months, even years.

I find a plant based lifestyle makes the digestion process flow much easier. I find that when you eat "green", it takes your body a fraction of the time to process the food you eat and to get rid of it. I found that the weight comes off easier and that you feel better. I am a living proof of what the lifestyle did for me. I lost over 30 lbs in keeping the plant based lifestyle.

I was determined to get my weight down. I tried starvation, the Adkins diet, and diet pills. You name it, I tried it. I just couldn't keep the weight off. I then had an "aha" moment. It was the food I was eating. I went to a plant based lifestyle and the weight fell off and stayed off. I have a new energy level and do not feel sluggish and out of breath like I used to be.

I think the Jewish lifestyle of eating Kosher also enables a person to eat healthier. If you do eat Kosher meat, it comes from a cow or chicken that has been fed organically without hormones or preservatives. According to Jewish laws, the animal must be slaughtered by a ritual slaughterer and with a process that prohibits causing any pain to animals.

In the book "To Be a Jew", author Rabbi Hayim Halevy Donin suggests that the dietary laws are designed as a call to holiness. The ability to distinguish between right and wrong, good and evil, pure and defiled, the sacred and the profane, is very important in Judaism. Imposing rules on what you can and cannot eat ingrains that kind of self control, requiring us to learn to control even our most basic, primal instincts.

The reason I think this is such an important part of the equation in my journey is because there was a time that I was winded going up and down stairs and I was tired of being sick and tired. I knew I needed to change if I wanted to be around another fifty years. I tried exercising but to be honest, it did not help because I never ate right. You can not feel good about yourself eating foods that are not good for you.

I remember listening to a tape by a well-known motivational fitness guru who took a test to determine his age by the lifestyle that he followed. He scored an age of 45, and he was 45. He thought that was strange because he exercises daily, felt phenomenal and thought he should have scored a younger age. When he first took the test, one of the questions was, "do you eat fresh vegetables daily" and he marked the answer as "no". He went back and retook the test, and this time checked "yes". The test came back this time as being 10 years younger. I cannot say how eating a vegetarian diet helped my energy, my stamina, and overall feeling good but it sure beats being tired and lethargic.

I remember in 2015 going to an open house at a health clinic where they were offering to take your heart rate, blood pressure, etc. Everything came back normal. Then I got on the scale and did a body fat analysis. The nurse looked me right in the eyes and said, you are obese. I thought she was the devil!

I was really taken back by that. I am just shy of 6 feet tall, and weighed 228 lbs. I considered myself skinny but she didn't agree. I said thank you and told everyone how wrong she was. Weeks later I realized she was right.

I believe that vegetables and fruit are the key to a long life. How did I get into this lifestyle? My wife, Donna. Soon after my wake-up call at the health clinic, she heard about a cardiologist who was speaking at a local event. The cardiologist, Dr. Joel Kahn, said that when a person comes to him, they have already had a heart attack. He suggests his patients adapt a plant based lifestyle to help reverse heart disease before you see him. More specifically, he tells them to stay away from meat, and eat a diet consisting of vegetables, and fruits.

I was not sure why this is important but he made a convincing argument that this is the cause all the health related issues in our country. In other countries, they don't have these kind of problems because they don't eat the processed and junk food that we American's eat. They don't have the sugars, the high fructose, the antibiotics and all the artificial stuff that we put into our food to preserve it. They don't allow the preservatives and all those chemical additives. Most countries won't even buy the food we sell in the United States.

Dr. Kahn believes that we can totally do away with type 2 diabetes and most of our heart disease, if we just ate a plant based diet. I was hooked. I do not want to see you as a patient, Joel Kahn. MD!

Dr. Kahn takes a holistic approach to heart disease, and is the author of several books including, "Dead Execs Don't Get Bonuses: The Ultimate Guide to Surviving Your Career with a Healthy Heart", "Your Whole Heart Solution", "Vegan Sex: Vegans Do It Better", and "The No B.S. Diet". (www.drjoelkahn.com)

Chapter 12

IT ALL CAME TOGETHER

After I incorporated every facet of my financial recovery and Jewish Journey into my daily life, it took ten years, but I was able to overcome my debt and find my authentic self.

Soon after I attended T. Harv Eker's "Millionaire Mind Intensive" seminar, I found that I had a passion for trading in worldwide option exchanges and turned this into a very lucrative passive income stream. I read every book I could get my hands on, and worked with well-known coaches who were experts in trading. I was able to start applying what I learned in 2008 when I worked part time as an intern at the New York Stock Exchange. I took it upon myself to travel around the world to observe foreign stock exchanges. I set up appointments in Hong Kong, Sydney, Israel, and elsewhere.

As I got comfortable trading on the world markets, I came up with a trading system I called, "Follow the DAX". I would take the stocks being traded in Europe, stocks like Apple, Google, Priceline, Visa, Mastercard, Netflix, Facebook, etc. I monitored the stocks on the Swiss exchange and traded the stock in the United States accordingly. For example, if Apple dropped 3% in Europe, I would buy Apple in the U.S. markets to do the same thing. The system worked remarkably well and this became an alternative income for me.

I developed several other trading systems, the "Donnalan Group", the "Friday Only Trading System", and several others. I go into specific details about these trading systems in my next book, "My Options Journey", which will be published in spring of 2019.

In the meantime, you can follow me on my Facebook page, https://www.facebook.com/AuthorAlanAsp/.

www.ingramcontent.com/pod-product-compliance
Lightning Source LLC
LaVergne TN
LVHW020439080526
838202LV00055B/5262